Inventory

poems by

Stacie M. Kiner

Finishing Line Press
Georgetown, Kentucky

Inventory

For Dianne
For John

Copyright © 2021 by Stacie M. Kiner
ISBN 978-1-64662-585-7 First Edition
All rights reserved under International and Pan-American Copyright Conventions. No part of this book may be reproduced in any manner whatsoever without written permission from the publisher, except in the case of brief quotations embodied in critical articles and reviews.

ACKNOWLEDGMENTS

Deep thanks and regard to the editors of the publications where these poems were published:

Charlotte Poetry Review: "Mercy," "The Place Where You Left Off"
The Comstock Review: "Lament"
Ekphrastic Review: "The Man in My Mango Tree"
The Lavender Review: "Letters of My Dead"
The Madison Review: "God and Morphine"
The Meridian Anthology of Contemporary Poetry: "Colorado Springs, 1967"
Panoply: "Inventory"
Sun Dog: The Southeast Review: "Cottonwood Lane"
SWWIM: "All the Ways to Want Things"

Kind thanks to: The Courtyard, Stuart, FL., and The Vermont Studio Center, where many of these poems were completed, and to: Lenny DellaRocca, Howard Diamond, Lucia Leao, Michael O'Mara, Kodi Miller, Johannah Olsher, Dianne I. Rosenberg and Patricia Whiting.

Publisher: Leah Huete de Maines
Editor: Christen Kincaid
Cover Art: Stacie M. Kiner
Author Photo: Dr. Blaise Allen
Cover Design: Dianne I. Rosenberg

Order online: www.finishinglinepress.com
also available on amazon.com

Author inquiries and mail orders:
Finishing Line Press
PO Box 1626
Georgetown, Kentucky 40324
USA

Table of Contents

Inventory 1

All the Ways to Want Things 3

God and Morphine 5

Letters of My Dead 7

Nothing Spared 9

The Last Trip 11

Noche Buena Miami, FL. 2010 13

The Only Faith 14

Continuous 16

Weather and Misunderstanding 17

The Way Love Sometimes 19

Gravity 21

Colorado Springs, 1967 22

Parachute 24

Winding the Watch 26

Linville Falls 28

Aria 29

Mercy 30

The Place Where You Left Off 31

Cottonwood Lane 32

Lament 33

Venetian Pool 35

The Man in My Mango Tree 36

Inventory

> *The surface of things*
> *can barely hold…what is under them.*
> —Eavan Boland

As a child,
I parked my broken bike
in the garage,
believing it would be
fixed overnight.

Wasn't this the way
you died,
believing you
would be fixed
in the morning?

Your ashes sit
in a small cardboard box
in our air-conditioning closet.

Some of you
I buried
with sunflowers
in my garden,
some I carry
in my backpack.

Now that your home is rain,
I don't know where
you live.
I don't know
if the scales on which
lives are weighed
would show you happy
but there you were,
sitting in the sun,
your aide's phone
in your shirt pocket
playing Sinatra.

Now that your envelope
of silence
will never be opened,

what did it take
to not become
tomorrow?

What do I do now
with daffodils,
their thick, milky stems
cut from our garden
wrapped in damp paper towel and foil
for my favourite teachers?

I came to see you
stored like luggage
emptied
after a long trip,
your third home
in one year

sitting in a row
of wheelchairs aligned like planets
revolving around a television set,
wearing someone else's shoes.

After you died
and we became closer,
I wondered;
is catastrophe
simply a place
water finds
its way through?

Is this what we are—
a cracked slate roof
in a home with bowls
filling with rain?

With nothing left
but surrender,
how far
do we have to fly
before
we touch ground?

All the Ways to Want Things

> *"... this voice was never mine, nor even yours."*
> —Lawrence Raab

Our world slowly spinning
unbuttons itself;
this is a difficult home.

And you
the reason for this telling
the way memory
and subtraction fool us—
a sun-warmed Key lime
sliced in half
its juice on your tongue.
Your husband gone
taking your child for shoes.
And you, eyes closed;
falling straight
to the heart of God—

the smooth slide into the back
of a cooled taxi's leather seat.

But maybe everyone is always
almost drowning;
and maybe this is all
you want to be.

Like the mailbox as a child
I stuffed with snow,
you could not receive a thing.

Stitching back up
the blood you lose
each month,
forgetting the march
of happiness
right down to your toes.
Forgetting our world still spins
with its nature of hope.

So I ask for everything—

I don't know where to stop.
Hands tight on a wheel
one fine turn away—

and all the ways to want things;
and all the things
we shouldn't want.

God and Morphine

I broke my leg once,
walked into the street
between a car and a van
that didn't stand still.
The van's bumper scooped me up
like a bull's horns
on a matador's thigh
and sent me flying.

Sex became difficult.
All I could do
was float on the bed
dazed
telling her about Macbeth
while drawing crazy hearts
on her cheek
with a lipstick brush.

Her husband spent his time
in the kitchen,
separating frozen French fries,
removing them from the box
and placing them in the oven.
After the fries
were done,
he would pull out
Civil War maps and memorabilia
and wonder who God was,
while he tacked the maps
to the living room wall.
He would read about Grant and Lee
while drawing lines on his maps—
moving men long buried
in the Tennessee earth.

Later, we'd emerge to hear
how many thousands of men
died at Manassas,
how many days it took supplies
to get from Vicksburg
to the troops,

and how no morphine was left
before the war's end.
This went on for months.
The Civil War quietly playing
in the background
while men long buried
filtered through the room
past the locked door,
asking questions about
someone named God,
and why it took so long
to get supplies from Vicksburg
to the troops.

I haven't seen them now
for a long time.
And I wonder
how many lines
he's drawn on his maps,
but mostly,
who is sharing their bed.

Letters of My Dead

Letters of my dead
carry leaves and dirt
to school
in pencil boxes;
miniature coffins
preparing us for lives
held underwater,
sand and earth
and beach chairs
washed away.

Twisting open Bahamian shutters
in a room in our favourite hotel,
I fold the map of your body
into my back pocket,
trying to explain
pull of earthly tethers,
flight of soul from matter.

If I were mathematical
I could calculate the meaning
of nights like these,
unredeemed
rapture and grief entwine
as everything falls from the ledge
of a tilting planet

how far can wind carry you
when you won't let go?

Our world is held
in buckets of water
that fill on the floor

as clouds cast
judgement
overhead.

The dead—
where aren't they?

As your body pulls away
from itself,
birds in a Cornell box
sing of assembled sculpture,
subway tokens, compasses.

Listen—
each life becomes
beaten to a thinness
radiant as air.

Take comfort in this

past to which you never
have to return,
shoebox tossed to the wind

and if there is any
innocence left

punch holes
in its lid
to keep it alive.

Nothing Spared

Do you wish
to pin my arms
above my head,
long kiss
uncoiling
both of us
never
coming back?

Is this what you do
when you don't want
a body
any longer?

Or when your body
decides it wants
its own words—

a language of pleasure
it will not share
with your
crooked
heart

that can't be trusted,
murmurs in blood,
sleeps a beat too long,
wants what it wants
and all you want is to give it

until heaven sends itself
in facsimile—
filling the sky
with more blue.

You, a woman of forty-two
after many husbands
and one wife
sleep alone
with a stuffed bear.

If I throw my net
on a place no longer able
to be pinned down
and held beneath glass
would I still catch you?

The world was made
to be cruel, broken

and love
is such
a small,
hard word.

The Last Trip

It takes so long
to throw some things away.

The fig jam
now hard to open
but still somehow good,
the car that tried
but couldn't
make it up
the hill.

I wish no one
would remember

the Christmas tree
that had to be perfect,
the child stepping outside
to scream,
the woman dressing
in the driveway
to get away.

Is everything for sale
when you become
a sacrifice?

At the top of the list
of all you have to lose,

watch
as clouds form a house,
watch
as they blow away.

You could say
it's temporary
but it's not,
even graves are alive;
the grass trimmed weekly.

As our world fills with things

that open and close
and soil is
passed from mourner
to mourner

wouldn't it be beautiful
and wouldn't you wish

for one wooden match
to burn it all down?

Noche Buena Miami, FL. 2010

Wasn't that the night
*someone left the cake out
in the rain?*

Your father's homemade
Cuban pork roast,
and Celia Cruz and Donna Summer.

Your tío from L.A.
called me *Jennifer* all night
then gave me his card,
in case, you never know.

We got drunk
danced and kissed
in the kitchen

while your father,
certain that
your mother,

passed out and asleep
on the floor
between the bed
and the wall,
had finally left him,

walked around and around
the outside of the house,
calling for her to come home.

Now, he tells me
*everything's gone
to shit back in L.A.,*

*Stern's sons
ran the famous
barbecue
into the ground and,
you can't even smoke
in Macarthur Park.*

The Only Faith

As past tense fades
into lasting kiss,
I think of old flashcubes
spinning on top of a camera,
turning you into light.

What becomes of appetites
impossible to comfort?
Do you remember
scotch and ice
sliding down my arm,
melting between
your clenched teeth?

It was easy after that,
turning you into an altar—
believing sex
was the only faith.

Our bodies tearing
at their own tethers;
I thought we'd learn
to fly.

Now, I want you
where the dead are.
In a dark earth
falling through my life,
forgotten, but not;
gone
but here;

so I can carry you
through the end
of every day
into another,
send you out
in a skiff
of battered wood—

even if love

has no compass
it has a place to go,

sailing into any past
lashed to promises
laid end to end
looking for some
east or west
far enough
to not
call home.

Continuous

> *Le monde n'est que de*
> *rein, mais le nullite*
> *se voit encore a travers.*
>   —Paul Valery

This is a hard
gravel life
where dreams are measured
against loss,
things fall through
a body
like love or sand
or the need for one thing
inside the need for another.
As if Valery were right,
the world is made from nothing
but the nothing shows through.

Will I too turn
into nothing—
slip into
silken loam of night
break my weave
unravel my heart,
my body, floating—
a body of water
and no more?

As everything moves
against forgetting,
will the river
keep count
on my mud heart,
remembering the body
I was part of

wandering, lost
unfastened?

Weather and Misunderstanding

Kicked dirt
of promises,
howl of prairie
in a Midwest city,
long, dry roll
of tumbleweed

as the past unwinds
cracked
and sepia—

I can't stop the branch
scrape on bone,
thin twine of memory
keeping it together

I didn't create the weather.

I give back
your photograph
of the farm
and leave
everything else—

poems I painted on the wall
maps of years
roads
freeways
I took
to nowhere.

I'll drop you a line
sometime,
tell you I couldn't be
contented
with a contented heart,

how much water
we need to survive,
how roads in moonlight
still pass

the same
farms and fields
even if we
are not on them. Water

runs over this now.
Your hands, your face,
submerged
your name, with water
fading.

I'm sorry. I'm trying to find
a voice
as hard and bitter
as water
that filled the locks
every winter

when the canal
was drained.

The Way Love Sometimes

As our world
dissolves
in rain,

I wonder
how much
can rivers swallow,
how much
of my life
do I have
to remember—
the half that is gone
or the half I think
remains?

Are you part
of the world
that dies
and never
comes back?

On a balcony,
a woman
blew kisses across
a parking lot—

now it's easier
to predict weather
than to know
what she was thinking.

Wanting
so many things:
the birds
in my mouth
to lift my heart,
the bowl of sadness
to stop filling
with rain.

Is this the person

I meant to become,
wishing
one year over
before
another's begun?

Gravity
> *Over me...a spell of shining.*
> —James Merrill

Loosening the dress
of air
drifting in the helium
of desire
kisses assume
rococo proportions
as clouds unravel
beneath us.

In a borrowed brass bed
bliss becomes stories
our bodies tell
in different ways.

Blessing this life
and everything in it
must we
apologize for want—
does abundance always
equal sorrow?

What of the pleasure
revolving around
leaving your life
behind

stepping into tinsel
wishing for wings—

a spell of shining?

Colorado Springs, 1967

Thrown from a car window
into enormous sky
you thought you could fly
like this
forever—
but forever
takes decades to resolve.

You were dying
and everyone came to see you
except me

not knowing
how to turn the record over
on the player you bought me

or where Colorado Springs
even was.

Wrapped in a white blanket
lowered out the back of an airplane,
your shaved head explained
a vice-president
learning to tie his shoes,
crawling up steps
in the house on Elmwood Avenue—
your silence was rage
until rage could be spoken.

Deep sea fishing off Cape Ann
we ran into a school of mackerel;
iridescent lures calling rainbow fish
were prisms under water.

Living with less and less
I kept adding more string,
believing if my kite
could touch the clouds
you would not un-spool.

In a world made

of yellow and blue
around which our lives spin

how small
but great things are.

Parachute

> *I have woven a parachute out of everything broken.*
> —William Stafford

I wonder if he traces
his path from a childhood
spent lifting last winter's logs

to a life then spent
putting things under weight,
so they wouldn't fly away?

His days now
held together
with holes full of rain
woven through seasons
of ice and thaw

as long days of measure
finally end,
as everything once whole
is halved
then halved again.

I consider
the creep of finality:
one day
he stopped getting
what he wanted
then stopped caring
then stopped noticing

slippers,
sweatpants
never worn,
now worn all day.

All pressed and properly
hung slacks
become
admonishments
accommodating
absence.

I am all
he has left.

As each day's
stitch
unravels

trees now form
a perfect sky

into which
he falls.

Winding the Watch

My father tries
to wind the watch
that doesn't wind.
Isn't this what happens,
resuscitating time,
wanting to wind
a watch
that doesn't wind?

Covering mirrors
in the gradual
dismantling
of his brain

the reversal
and correction
of clouded desires,
call and recall
of all that's bloody
and wonderful
simultaneously—

memory
still roped
but frayed
at both ends.

I lean in
to the silent wood
of his heart—

moving him
from home to home
removing glass
from frames
then frames,
then photos.
Each place equals less:

clothes left in closets,
deck shoes on curbs,

cameras, yearbooks,
placed in a wheelchair
and rolled to the car;
I couldn't
carry
it all.

What is left to do
but welcome the machinery,
plowing the path to nothing
damaged
but still translucent

a surface
under too much weight,
when memory
only equals
atonement?

As silence is splayed
between us
how much is imagined;

our lives happening
under our lives
with water
streaming through?

Inevitably,
what territory
is not childhood

the hard candy
nothing
can remove—

as we pull up
the earth
and call it home?

Linville Falls

What is amazing
is anything
survived.

The rib joint
at the foot
of The Smokies
where we ate
one
of our many
last meals.

The jam
(that outlived us)
bought
from a table
in the bend
of the mountains,
where we
placed our money
in a dill pickle jar.

You may say
falling
from here
is good

so many
clouds
to hold us—

pretending,
with each creak
of the teak chair

everything
was fine.

Aria

Looking for you
on a beach
after an argument,
I mistook you for
the shadow
of a pelican
flying low
overhead.

In Paris
we watched a film
of a man writing
with pen and inkwell
in the rain.

Isn't this
what disappearing is—
holding our wings
in

as we
try
to fly?

Mercy

The year has worn itself out.
Centuries of rain fall
the city cannot hold.
Curtains fill by the open window
breathing in and out;
beauty
that rises and falls
and calls you to it.
I let this wash over me
my childhood in Africa
one endless procession
of dust and rice—
eventually,
we all get our due.
Numbers and faces converge
with memories of our little deaths;
one long row of multiplication—
face upon face upon face
that equals nothing and says,
this is where grace ends.
Love, like a junk
set out to sea and sunk;
letters that arrive
long after someone has died.
But sorrow isn't so bad really,
the song birds sing every day,
the dust that was you. Still
we stir sweetness
from the bottom
as snow falls on the seaboard,
falls on a forest at night;
smoothing and quieting the land
as it rolls in its bed,
pulling snow over its shoulders
and here, down here,
morning falls with copper and light
and all the rooftops remind you
of a Hopper painting
soft and blue and yellow
dreaming its way out of sleep.
A light turned on in the farmhouse,
sugar tossed in a grave,
mercy left in the land.

The Place Where You Left Off

Someday, we will know for sure we are alone.
—Richard Hugo

This is the hardest thing.
The taste of nothing in your mouth
an absence of flavor that speaks forgetfulness—
language only water knows,
it swallows; and is forgiven. Still

you want something else to speak for you.
Some repertoire of longing—
a last kiss burning in your mouth,
a lone bird screaming across the sky. This

is the way something begins to bleed.
Water seeps into a life.
With time, memory like earth softens,
and is buried deeper then deeper. So

fall out of love
with everything in this world
that won't work—
the boat that takes on water
even as it sits in the yard. There's

a freight, darling
rumbling lies laid out coast to coast
as full of coal as sorrow
tumbling down some chute;
bound for forever
where any place can be

the place where you left off.

Cottonwood Lane
for Mark

When I left
and took the train up the coast
you moved to Cottonwood Lane—
calling for me
to come home.

It was settled:
I would learn how to be a woman,
a fruit, halved,
bleeding down the pages
of your life
and calling your name

until all that was left
was the howling sound of hearts
like buildings collapsing—

the empty click of a key
on a wooden dresser.

Once, when we slept
in the desert
outside Las Vegas
and the coyotes came,
you held me close in our tent.
Now in a dream I phone you
then remember
you are corn

long since sifted
through my hands—

turquoise and wind,
and all things
that begin
and never end.

Lament

> *One thing about the living*
> *sometimes a piece of us*
> *Can stop dying for a moment.*
> —W.S. Merwin

That wasn't so bad.
Spinning her on the dance floor
brushing hair from her eyes.

There's a strange thing clouds do
the way they pour into
and out of each other,
the way I threw her out
and she came back—
some hidden compass telling her
no then, alright then,
better than alright.

This is what I want
her on her knees—
to be able to say, have to say:
Enough. No more.
I want to take it and take it.
And have you take it and take it.

> I want to turn over
> the earth of her heart.
> Bury something deep
> in her bones.

Something soft and smooth;
somehow lovely—
a heron in an estuary at twilight.
Wading sandbar to sandbar.
Mangrove to mangrove.

> If you wait long enough
> you'll get water.
> If you run your tongue over this
> you'll get salt.

At dawn, when the sky breaks into pieces,
breaks into its own weather—

I'll tell her there is more than weather
to hold her.

If she opens her palm
I'll pour sand into her.
Something amber and golden—

a pitcher pouring light
out of light.

www.ingramcontent.com/pod-product-compliance
Lightning Source LLC
LaVergne TN
LVHW041555070426
835507LV00011B/1099